Cambridge English Readers

Level 1

Series editor: Philip Prowse

Bad Love

Sue Leather

CAMBRIDGE
UNIVERSITY PRESS

University Printing House, Cambridge CB2 8BS, United Kingdom

One Liberty Plaza, 20th Floor, New York, NY 10006, USA

477 Williamstown Road, Port Melbourne, VIC 3207, Australia

4843/24, 2nd Floor, Ansari Road, Daryaganj, Delhi – 110002, India

79 Anson Road, #06–04/06, Singapore 079906

Cambridge University Press is part of the University of Cambridge.

It furthers the University's mission by disseminating knowledge in the pursuit of education, learning and research at the highest international levels of excellence.

www.cambridge.org
Information on this title: www.cambridge.org/9780521536530

First published 2003
Reprinted 2017

Printed in the United Kingdom by Hobbs the Printers Ltd

A catalogue record for this publication is available from the British Library

ISBN 978-0-521-53653-0 Paperback

Contents

People in the story

Flick Laine: a detective in the Denver Police Department
Judy Kaplan: Flick's friend and a doctor at the University of Colorado Hospital, Denver
Leo Cohn: Chief of the Denver Police Department and Flick's boss
Danny Reno: a young detective
Jack Daly: a doctor at Judy's hospital
Sandy Baker: a woman from Aspen, Colorado

Places in the story

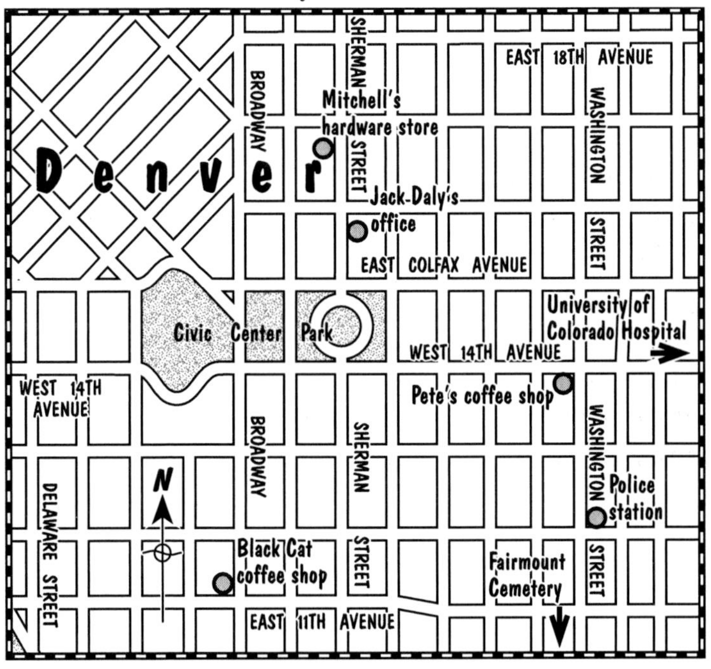

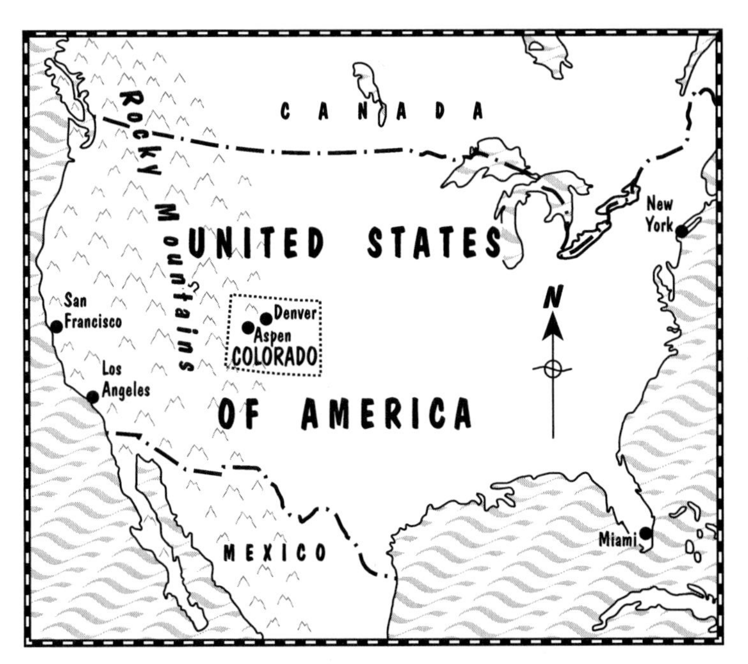

Chapter 1 *The doctor*

I met Dr. Jack Daly in August.

It was a Saturday afternoon. I was at a party in Denver at my friend Judy Kaplan's house. We were in the backyard and it was hot. It's always hot in the summer in Denver. It was a good party. About fifty people were there and there were drinks and good food.

I walked around the backyard and talked to people. I had a drink and tried some food. And then, I met Jack Daly.

"Hi," he said. He had black hair and blue eyes. "My name's Jack. Jack Daly."

"Hi," I said. "I'm Flick. Flick Laine."

We talked a little. He told me he was a doctor and that he worked at the University of Colorado Hospital in Denver.

"What about you?" he asked me.

"I'm a detective," I said. "Denver Police Department."

"Oh, a cop!" he said with a smile. He had very white teeth.

I smiled back at him. "Yeah," I said, "a cop."

"So where's your police car?" he said.

"That's my car, over there," I said. "It's the red 1957 Chevrolet."

"A '57 Chevy! That's a beautiful car!" he said. "I love old Chevies."

We talked some more about cars. Then, "OK," he said, "now tell me more about *you*."

"Well," I said, "my first name's . . . er . . . Felicity." I laughed.

"Felicity?"

"Yes," I said. "My dad liked it. But please call me Flick."

We talked a little more. After some minutes, he said, "Well, I'm leaving now, Flick. Can I see you again some time?" He smiled again. He had a beautiful smile.

I smiled too. "OK. Sure," I said and gave him my phone number. He walked slowly out of the backyard and I watched him. "Tall and dark. Nice!" I thought.

Later, after the party, I talked to Judy about Daly.

"Tell me about the doctor," I said.

"Jack Daly?" Judy looked at me. "He's a very good doctor. All the rich people go to him; you know, movie stars, sports stars. He's famous at the hospital." Judy is a doctor too, at the university hospital.

"Oh, famous, is he?" I said. "I don't often like famous people."

Judy looked into my eyes. "Oh, come on, Detective Laine," she said, "you like *him*! I watched you with him. All the women like him."

* * *

The next Monday, Jack Daly phoned me.

"I want to talk to you about something," he said. "How about coffee?"

"Sure," I said.

"Friday, eleven o'clock at the Black Cat coffee shop on Broadway?"

"OK," I said. "See you on Friday."

But I never saw Jack Daly again. On Wednesday my

boss, Leo Cohn, chief of the Denver Police Department, called me into his office.

"Dead?" I said. "Jack Daly?"

"Did you know him?"

"Not very well," I said. "I met him at a party four days ago."

"Oh," said Cohn. "Well, now he's dead."

"How?" I asked. "Was it at the hospital?"

Cohn stood by his desk with some papers in his hand. He was a thin man who worked too much. He never sat down.

"No," said Leo. "He died in his office downtown. Reno's there now." Reno was Danny Reno, a detective in the Denver Police Department. "He thinks Daly killed himself."

"Killed himself?" I felt cold.

"Reno thinks so," said Leo.

"But Daly phoned me on Monday, Leo," I said. "He wanted to talk to me about something – this Friday. A man who wants to kill himself doesn't do that!"

"Well, Reno says he's dead and he has a gun in his hand," he said. "Reno's waiting for you. Go and have a look. The office is at 1237 Sherman."

I looked at my watch. It was nine o'clock. I took my car key and my gun and got into my red Chevrolet. I drove to Daly's office on Sherman.

Chapter 2 *Dead*

It was a hot day. It was late August and, at nine o'clock in the morning, it was hot. I drove fast and turned the radio on. I like to listen to music in the car. This time it was Norah Jones, singing *Cold Cold Heart*. But it was no good. I only thought about Jack Daly. "I want to talk to you about something," he said. I thought about the coffee and the conversation we didn't have.

Fifteen minutes later I was at his office. The first thing I saw was his dead body, lying over his desk. The gun was in his hand.

I didn't speak for a minute. I often see dead bodies. It's my job. But they're not often people I know. I turned away from Daly's body and looked at the room. The office was big and looked expensive; the office of a rich doctor. There were some pictures of American cities on the wall: Los Angeles, Miami, San Francisco.

And behind Daly's body, out the window, was Denver. It was twenty past nine in the morning and Denver looked like it always looked. A man was dead, but the city didn't change. That's how it is.

Then I turned to Danny Reno. There were two police officers with him.

"I want photos of everything," I said to Reno. "And can you take some fingerprints of the room and the gun?"

"The gun?" asked Reno. "Don't you think he killed himself, Detective?"

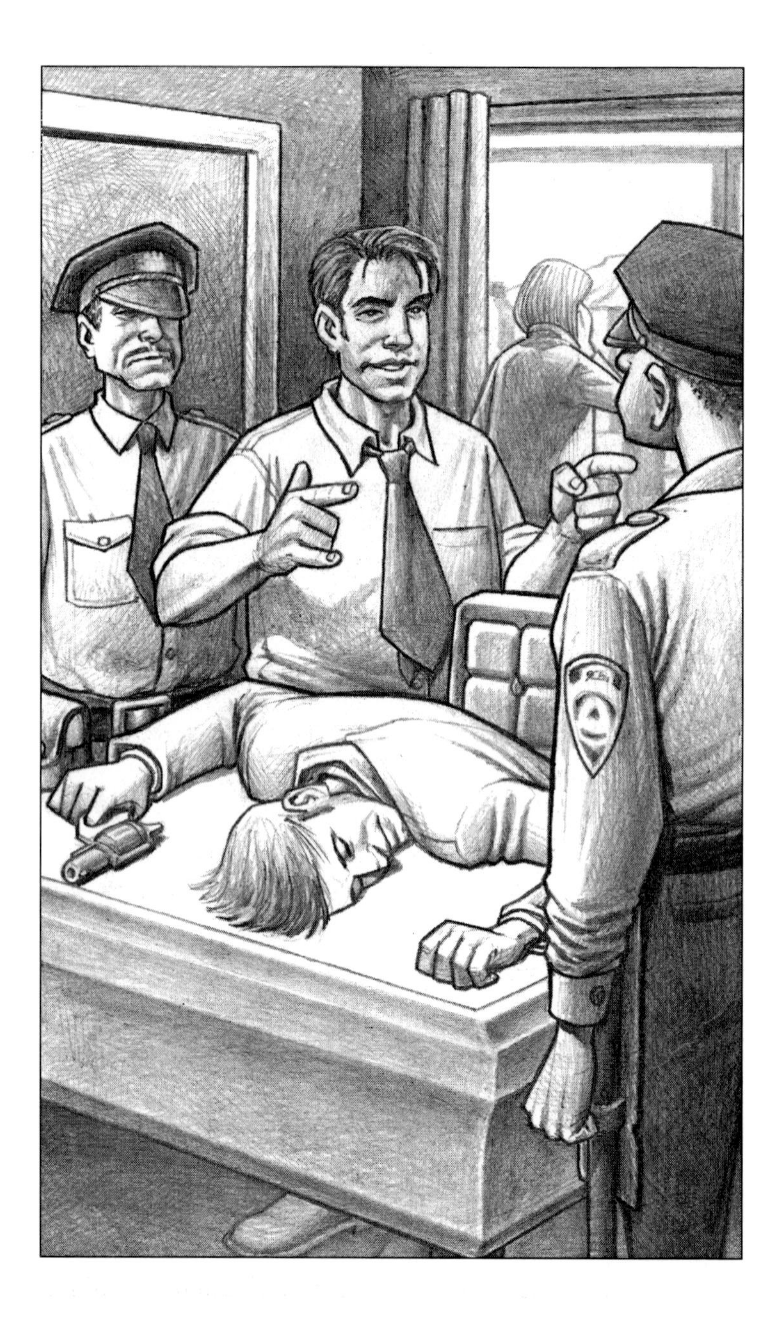

I looked back at Daly's body. The gun was in his right hand. I thought about Judy's party and Jack Daly with a glass in his hand. His *left* hand.

"Um," I said, "I think Jack Daly was *left*-handed."

Reno just looked at me. He was about twenty-four with very black hair and Italian good looks. He wasn't very tall and he ate too much. But he was a good cop.

"Yes, Detective," he said. "We'll take the fingerprints right now."

"Who found the body?" I asked.

"Mark Johnson," said Reno. "He cleans the office."

"Where is he?" I asked.

"He's in the next room. He's waiting for you."

I talked to the cleaning man, Mark Johnson. He was a twenty-year-old student at the University of Colorado. He cleaned offices to make a little money.

Johnson cleaned six offices. That Wednesday morning,

he opened Dr. Daly's office at about eight-fifteen and found him. Dead. Then he phoned the police.

"What do you know about Dr. Daly?" I asked.

"Not much," he said. "I sometimes saw him and said 'Good morning'. I thought he was a nice guy."

"Yeah," I thought. "Jack Daly was a nice guy."

"Can I go now?" asked Johnson.

"Sure," I said, "but are you leaving Denver?"

"No," Johnson answered.

"Good," I said. "Call me if you think of anything important."

Johnson told Reno where he lived and then he left. I sat and thought. I only met Dr. Jack Daly that one time. And it was a short meeting. But I didn't think that he killed himself.

OK. He didn't kill himself. So, who did kill him?

Chapter 3 *Questions*

An hour after I talked to Mark Johnson, I was at the University of Colorado Hospital. I got out of the Chevy and walked to the front door. I asked to see Dr. Judy Kaplan.

I waited for about ten minutes. Then Judy came.

"Hi, Flick!" she said. "What are you doing here?"

I didn't answer her. I just asked, "Do you have time for coffee?"

"Something wrong?" she asked.

Again, I didn't answer her.

We went down to the hospital cafeteria. We sat at a small table near the window and drank our coffee. I looked at Judy. I didn't know what to say. I looked out the window at the trees and flowers in the hospital garden.

Then I told Judy about Jack Daly.

"Dead? What . . . ? How . . . ?" said Judy. She closed her eyes.

"I don't know," I said. "He died in his office. I saw him this morning. It looks like he killed himself, but *I* don't think so."

She opened her eyes again and looked at me. "So you think . . . ?"

"Well," I said, "I don't know."

Judy's face was white. We drank our coffee. We didn't say anything for a minute or two.

"Was Daly happy here?" I asked.

"I don't know," Judy answered. "I think so."

"When did he start at the hospital?" I asked her.

"Only about a year ago," she replied.

"Was there anybody here who didn't like him?" I asked.

"I don't think so," she said.

"And before he came here?"

"He was in Florida, I think," she said. "Miami."

I thought about the pictures on the walls of Daly's office. Yes, there was a picture of Miami.

"At a hospital there?" I asked.

"I don't know," she said. "Look, I'm sorry Flick, but I must go back to work."

Judy stood up and left. I went to the police station. I talked to Leo. I told him what I thought, that Daly didn't kill himself. I told him about the gun in his right hand.

"Well, all right," he said, "but you say Jack Daly was a nice guy. So why did somebody kill him?"

"Good question," I said. I didn't know the answer.

That evening I sat in my apartment and looked at Danny Reno's photos. I looked at Jack Daly's body. I looked and looked.

Then I heard the telephone. It was Reno.

"More news about Jack Daly's body," said Reno. "You were right, Detective. Jack Daly *was* left-handed. It was Daly's gun but it was in his right hand. He didn't kill himself. It was murder."

"Yeah," I said. "I thought so."

"We found a letter in Daly's office, too."

"A letter?"

"That's right," said Reno. "It just says, 'You are never going to forget Jeff Baker!'"

The next morning I met Danny Reno at our office and he gave me the letter. It was in big, black writing.

"Do you think it's important?" asked Reno.

"I don't know," I said. I thought about Jack Daly's phone call to me on Monday. Did Daly want to talk to me about the letter?

I read it again. "You are never going to forget Jeff Baker!"

"The letter was in this," said Reno. He gave me an envelope with Daly's name on it, but not the address of his office.

"Listen, Danny," I said, "I've got a job for you. I want you to look for Jeff Baker. How did Jack Daly know him? I'm sorry, it's not an easy job. There must be hundreds of Jeff Bakers in Colorado. You can start in Denver."

"Sure, Detective," said Reno. "Oh, and here's something about the gun." Reno gave me some papers and left my office.

I started to read. "The gun that killed Dr. Jack Daly," it said, "was a Ruger SP101 and it was Daly's gun. The killer shot the doctor, then cleaned the gun and put it into the dead man's hand."

OK. But where did the killer get Daly's gun? And how did he get into Daly's office? Who was Jeff Baker? And why did Daly want to talk to me?

I had a lot of questions, but no answers. It was the end of August and we didn't have anything. We had nothing on Jeff Baker and we knew nothing about who killed Jack Daly.

But then the month of August became the month of September, and the answers started to come.

Chapter 4 *The key*

One evening, two weeks after the murder, Mark Johnson, the office cleaning man, called me.

"Detective Laine," he said. "Can I see you?"

"Yes, Mr. Johnson. Sure. What about?"

"You know the Daly murder? Well, I thought of something. You told me to call."

"Good," I said. "Come to Pete's coffee shop near the police station on Washington."

An hour later, Mark Johnson and I were at a table at Pete's.

"It's about the key," said Johnson.

"The key?"

"Yeah, the key to the door of Dr. Daly's office."

"What about it?"

"On that Tuesday, the day before Dr. Daly . . . died," said the young man, "I opened the door to Dr. Daly's office and I left the key in the door like always."

"I started to clean the office," he said, "then I finished and wanted to close the door . . . but the key wasn't there."

"So what did you do?" I asked.

"I just closed the door to the office and went to clean the next office," he said. "That was the only thing to do. I'm sorry I didn't tell you . . . I just forgot."

"Did you find the key?"

"Yes," he said. "When I came back to Dr. Daly's office later, it was there again, in the door."

"And how long were you away?" I asked.

"About an hour," said Johnson.

An hour. "In an hour," I thought, "it's easy to go and make a second key. And then easy later to go into Jack Daly's office and get his gun."

"Do you still have your key?" I asked him.

"Yes, I do," he said. "Here it is."

Johnson put the key on the table. It was small and didn't look very important, but it was the only thing I had. I took it.

"Thank you very much, Mr. Johnson," I said.

Very early the next morning, I drove to Jack Daly's office and parked the Chevy on the street. I looked for a store, the kind of store where they make keys. A hundred meters down the street I saw it. It was a hardware store called Mitchell's. They made keys there.

Did Jack Daly's killer go to this store and make a second key to his office?

I opened the door and went in.

"Good morning," I said to the man in the store. "Are you Mr. Mitchell?"

He was about fifty-five. He wore a dirty brown T-shirt and he had a face like an angry dog. He didn't answer me.

I tried again. "Two weeks ago, on Tuesday morning," I said, "it was early, at about maybe eight-thirty, somebody came in here to make a key like this." I opened my hand; there was the key.

"We're not open, lady," he said. "You're too early." He turned away.

My police badge was in my hand. I looked at it and then I looked at him. "My name is Detective Laine. When you see this, Mr. Mitchell, you're open 24/7!" I shouted. "Understand?"

"Can I help you, Detective?"

I looked up and saw a big red-haired woman. "Mrs. Mitchell," I thought.

"I was here early that Tuesday," said the woman. "My husband was still in bed." She looked angrily at her husband, but she smiled at me.

The woman looked at the key. "Yes," she said. "It was a young woman, pretty, about twenty-five or twenty-six, I think . . . short brown hair."

"A woman!" I thought.

"Can you tell me any more about her?" I asked.

"No, nothing . . . sorry," she said.

I asked some more questions and about ten minutes later, I left the hardware store.

"Thanks for everything," I said to the woman, then turned to her husband, "and take it easy, Mr. Mitchell."

I smiled. It was a good morning's work.

Chapter 5 *The green Toyota*

The next day, Judy and I went to say goodbye to Jack Daly at Fairmount Cemetery. It was a warm day and the trees were still green. It was a beautiful, sad day.

Judy and I stood and watched. I looked at the people there. A lot of them were doctors and nurses from the hospital. Jack Daly didn't have any family. His mother and father were dead, and he didn't have any brothers or sisters. There were some friends, many of them young women.

"Look at all these women," I said to Judy.

"Jack Daly was a ladies' man," she said. "He always had a lot of girlfriends!"

After it was finished, we started to walk away. But then, I saw a pretty young woman of about twenty-five. She had short brown hair.

"Who's that?" I asked Judy. "Is she from the hospital?"

"I don't think so," she answered. "I don't know her . . ."

Just then, the young woman started to walk away, fast. She walked to a green car – a Toyota.

"Listen," I said to Judy, "I'll see you later. I'm going to talk to her. I want to know who she is."

I left Judy. I walked fast too, but the young woman got into her Toyota and drove away.

I got into the Chevy and started to drive behind her. But she drove very fast. There were a lot of cars on the Denver streets and then, after some minutes, I wasn't behind the green Toyota anymore.

PKY-2397

The only thing I had was Colorado PKY 2397, the number on the back of the car.

I stopped and called Danny Reno. I told him about the car and the number.

Five minutes later, Danny called back. He was happy.

"Detective Laine," he said, "good news! The car's driver is Sandy Baker. She lives at 2327 Snowmass Street, Aspen, Colorado. I spoke to the Aspen Police Department. They're happy for you to talk to her."

I turned the Chevy around and got on the road to Aspen.

Chapter 6 *The sister*

Aspen is four hours from Denver by car. It's a beautiful town in the Rocky Mountains.

It was nine o'clock in the evening when I got to the house on Snowmass Street. I got out of the car and there was the green Toyota.

The young woman opened the door.

"Sandy Baker?" I said. "I'm Detective Flick Laine of the Denver Police Department. I'm here to talk about Jack Daly and why you were at Fairmount Cemetery today."

"Come in," she said. Her face was white.

We went into the living room.

"Please sit down, Detective Laine," she said. Then she spoke fast. "I'm sorry . . . um, I just wanted to see that he was dead, you see . . . for Jeff."

"Oh yeah?" I said. "Tell me about him."

"Jeff was my brother," she said. "He was a very good guy, and a very good football player . . . here's a picture of him."

I looked at the picture. It was of a smiling young man in a green, white and orange Miami Dolphins football shirt. He had brown hair and nice eyes, just like his sister.

"It was just him and me," she said. "Our mother and father died when we were young, and we lived with my aunt, my mother's sister, here in Aspen. She died about five years ago. Jeff was the only person I had in the world."

Sandy Baker started to cry.

"He played football in school here," she said. "Everyone said he was very, very good. A star football player."

"And then . . .?" I asked.

"After high school he went to college in Miami," said Sandy, and then she smiled, "but he just wanted to play football. In his second year, a man from the Miami Dolphins came to see him. He said that Jeff was a very good football player. But . . ."

"But what?"

"It was his back."

"His back?" I looked at her. She stopped crying, but her face was sad.

"Yes. Oh, at first it was nothing," she told me, "but then it got bad. He stopped playing football. He went to a doctor at the hospital."

"The doctor said, 'There's something wrong with your back, but I can help you'," said Sandy. "A month later the doctor 'helped' my brother with his back and then Jeff stopped walking too."

"Stopped walking?" I asked.

"That's right," she said.

"And the doctor was Dr. Jack Daly?" I asked.

"Yes," Sandy said. For a minute or two she said nothing more. Then she shouted, "My brother couldn't walk! He was twenty years old. Football was everything to him and he couldn't walk!"

"And so . . .?"

"Two months later, Jeff was still in the hospital," she said. "Every day they gave him pills but he didn't take them. He put them near his bed. Then one day he took all of them . . .," Sandy said.

"He killed himself?"

"Yes," she said. "Jeff killed himself."

For a minute she didn't speak. Then she said, "No. Jeff didn't kill himself. It was that stupid doctor! That stupid Jack Daly. Famous Dr. Jack Daly! He killed my brother!"

And then Jeff Baker's sister cried. She cried for a long time.

Chapter 7 *Bad love*

"And so you killed Jack Daly," I said.

Sandy Baker looked up. "What?"

"You killed him," I said.

The young woman looked at me. "No!" she shouted. "You think . . . ? No! *I* didn't kill him. That letter . . . I just wanted to tell him . . . to think about my brother. I wanted him never to forget my brother."

"Come on," I said. "You killed him!"

"I did *not* kill Jack Daly!" she shouted again. "Oh, I'm not sorry that he's dead, Detective Laine, but I didn't kill him!"

I looked at Sandy Baker. I don't know how, but I knew that she didn't kill Dr. Jack Daly. She loved her brother and she did something stupid. She sent Daly the letter that said, "You are never going to forget Jeff Baker!"

But Sandy Baker didn't kill Jack Daly. She hated him, but she wasn't a killer. So who was?

I got in the Chevy to drive back to Denver. It was very late. There were no cars on the road. I put the radio on. It was a song called *Bad Love*.

"Bad love . . . Bad love . . . No more bad love . . ." the music went.

I started to think. Mrs. Mitchell at the hardware store said, "It was a young woman, pretty, about twenty-five or twenty-six, with short brown hair." It didn't help much. A lot of women are about twenty-five or twenty-six with short brown hair – like Sandy Baker, like Judy . . .

Like Judy! And then it came to me . . . bad love! Judy loved Daly!

I thought about the day at the cemetery. "Jack Daly was a ladies' man," Judy said. "He always had a lot of girlfriends!" She was angry when she said that. And the day of the party at her house, when she said, "You like *him*. I watched you with him. All the women like him."

"Bad love . . ." the music went on.

She was Daly's girlfriend, but she wasn't the only woman for him. She loved Daly, but he didn't love her.

Then, Jack Daly wanted to talk to me, to go out with me! Judy thought the next new woman was me, her friend, and it was too much.

"Bad love . . ."

So that was it. Judy's love was bad love; the kind of love that makes you kill a person. I thought about the day at the hospital. The day when I told Judy I didn't think Jack Daly killed himself. I thought about Judy's white face and how she left quickly. Her face was white because she was afraid; because my friend, Judy Kaplan, killed Dr. Jack Daly!

I stopped the car. I was hot and tired. I felt bad. I stopped driving. I stopped and just sat there all night. I thought and thought and thought. At five o'clock in the morning, I knew what to do. I called Leo.

* * *

"Sad day," said Leo.

I didn't say anything. We just watched Reno take Judy Kaplan away from her house.

Then I got in my Chevy and I drove. OK, it's my job. The police often take people away from their houses, but they're not often people I know. I drove for a long time. I drove up into the Rocky Mountains. I drove until it was evening and the sky was orange and pink. I looked back at the city of Denver. It looked like it always looked. A man was dead and my friend killed him, but the city didn't change. That's how it is.

I just drove on until the sun went down over beautiful Colorado.